CW00429781

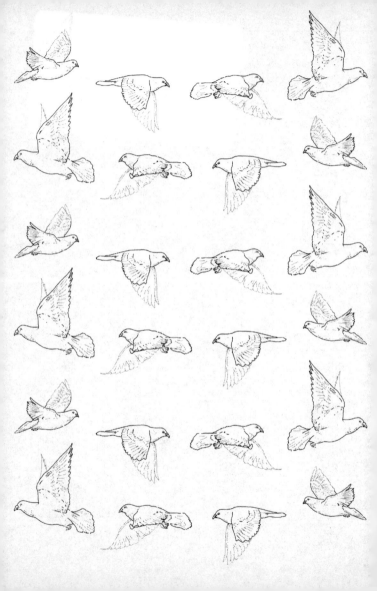

A MASSACRE OF HUMMINGBIRDS

Paul Blake

Stonewood
THUMBPRINTS

First published in 2016
by Stonewood Press
97 Benefield Road, Oundle PE8 4EU
books@stonewoodpress.co.uk
www.stonewoodpress.co.uk

All rights reserved
Poems © Paul Blake, 2016
The author asserts his moral right to be
identified as the author of this work

ISBN: 978-1-910413-13-5

Represented by Inpress
0191 230 8104
customerservices@inpressbooks.co.uk

Printed and bound in the UK by Imprintdigital, Exeter

Designed and typeset in Minion 10.5pt/12.5pt
by www.silbercow.co.uk
Cover illustration and endpapers by Martin Parker

This is the fifth book in the THUMBPRINT series

ACKNOWLEDGEMENTS

The poem 'Fall' was previously published in *Brittle Star*, and 'The Writing Master' in the anthology *Said and Done; New Writing from Brittle Star*. The poem 'Blackwater' and a version of the poem 'Winter Stars' were previously published as Members' Poems in *Poetry News*.

I am grateful to Mimi Khalvati and the members of her Advanced Poetry Workshop for encouragement and guidance over many years, and to the editors of *Brittle Star* and Stonewood Press in particular for their kind support of my work.

CONTENTS

BLACKWATER

A little after dawn, the estuary
still as a tin dish of milk

and the air astringent, like a pain so true
it must just be borne.

On the mudbank, brent geese
talk gentleness to one another

their soft round voices
like small observed thoughts afloat

over the gunmetal
of the flats, the sheepwool snags of mist.

To look out over water
is the sweetest beginning

even in memory
even when you lie between walls.

CREEK

Ours was a dormitory town. Its purlieus slept uneasily
in the choke-collar and chain of the new roads;
if it had dreams at night it never spoke of them.

Kept a Saxon church, toad-squat and stolid,
an old inn known for brawls, a whelk-stall in summer,
the glamorous rumour of a secret tunnel.

Its own idea of glamour was severely limited –
York-stone living room-bar, car that could do the ton.
There is no place better for growing a soul

than a town without one. That was our business
like all the young. We undertook the tricky navigation
of the ditch from its outflow below the school

as far as the station, braving the rattling flight
of dragonflies (the glittering Martian face,
the body rumoured one long deadly sting).

One place, and one place only in the right season
there grew yellow flag, a private treasure of gold.
And on the dry bank where we made our den

under cold thorn and wormy crab apple, packed
earth and root grew polished until they shone.
Who would have believed that mud could glow?

But when you went on, beyond the shelter of tree
and earth, under the iron of the railway towards flood
and sea wall and the shark-sleek easterlies

there would be mud that could eat a man, grey
as the tide's pelt, a carillon of rigging, curlews
calling a future too wide and sad for words.

WINTER STARS

You stood in the lane
crook-necked under the berg of night,
watching the Hunter stride
huge and glittering over the top of the hill.
When I shivered you opened
your jacket round me like a stolen cloud
reeking of gun oil, tobacco,
sweat and rabbit blood, your iron heat
freezing me in place.

In this clammy warmth
that chokes the throat of December
I think of those frosts, those skies;
of a time written in the language
of the winter stars, that language
in which every word is a verb.
You taught it to me:
to blaze; to be high;
to be splendid. To fall.

LEX(IS)

People say it can't be trusted –
language, that silvery disease –
but our anger is mostly because
it refuses to belong to us.
                    We remake it
in order to own it, yet still it escapes.

Where else will you put your faith –
in the body, a known traitor?
In the instabilities of thought
riddled with the black caves
                    the blind white fish
of deep grammar?

This is our inheritance, the taint
we can never scrub from our blood.
It is the only thing we will be given.
The small dipper of our tongues
                    negotiates
the cold burn of the world.

Ə [SCHWA]

Here is its sign – ə – an e doing handstands,
because although we say it with every breath
it does not have a letter in my language.

The sound of hesitation, uncertain, diffident,
creeping between the consonants like a cat
weaving between legs. Not the rough

breathing of 'ain, harsh as sand-laced wind,
nor the brisk closing of gates in a glottal stop.
Schwa, uh, er, huh. The thing it knows

is quietly moving on, its *raison-d'être*'s helping
things to flow. So we do: breathe and carry on
as we must, to get where we're going.

Uh, er, huh. Simple ə. And its sign, turned e,
might not seem right, too much the show-off
for this little sound, this sigh we make,

the body's opening to the wide world of air.
Yet surely something should do handstands,
at the sweetness of breath, that necessary

lovely thing, so rarely noticed when we
are at our ease, when every breath flows
freely. Something that remembers soul –

that soul is also a breath infusing us, a wind,
ruah, that blows through the towns of flesh.
Ruah, whose root also means perfume.

HELIOTROPE

This is the city of the Sun, the house of light
sheathed in white marble so she may admire her brilliance.

Underfoot, the city pavement gapes with the mouths
of those buried alive for daring to praise the moon.

Parching the soil, they swallow impartially
passing grease-stains of rain, the diamond spit

of lawn sprinklers outside the empty senate, the piss
of police dogs and bored soldiers in the square.

The dispossessed fold free newspapers, extolling
the brightness of the future, into hats to shade their eyes.

Plane and vine, orange and oleander have failed,
their scarecrow stumps scribbled with birdshit graffiti –

the only trickle of green, in courtyards or overhanging walls,
the murderous jasmine that strangles hearts by night.

FOR I SHALL CONSIDER THE CITY PIGEON

after Kit Smart

Forasmuch as their company are acolytes of a hungry god
For that they may be summoned by stale bread and grammarye
For they are sly, greedy, sex-obsessed and slightly mad
For the mighty accuse them of nurturing disease
For all their troubles have always come in flocks
For they have forgotten the land from which their forefathers
were driven
For the court of the crows has found them guilty
For they will tell you a very affecting story of their loss
For they shall be severally, and by parts, enumerated
For firstly their eyes, balas ruby, low-grade, *en cabochon*
For their beaks, the curve of silver ewers (Georgian)
For breathing in and out, the mask of a cyclist or a surgeon
Fourthly for voice a fountain, bronchitic wheeze
or orgasmic croon
For the neck the purple-green of oil leaks in the wet
For the back, mostly centuries of black time on slate
For the wings, stainable poor concrete and stormcloud violet
Further, the snap of small arms fire in their sounding flight
For their legs, branches of coral in tubercular twists
For their claws such chips of tarmac as star windscreen glass
For weaponry, an arse capacious and accurate at fifty paces
For their scent, musk of damp cellars and lock-up garages
For they are esteemed for their appreciation of art

For they are trafficked out of their own countries
For their estate is among the vermin
For the Ark has rested between their pinions
For they have shat upon the Scrolls of the Law
For they are more symbolic of the City than the ravens of the Tower
For they invoke the Blitz spirit but scarper when they see the cops
For they jeer at pigeon lofts and lead astray the racer
For they are prone to panic and mob rule
For they are the lost tribes of Israel
For they check themselves out in every mirror
For they keep a lodestone in their upper jaw
For they have the power of flight, but use it only when they must
For their enjoyments are meretricious and vulgar
For they believe the clatter of their wings brought down
                                        Jericho's wall
and they might shatter worlds but refrain out of courtesy
For they hold the chip to be the pinnacle of haute cuisine
For they secretly despise tourists
For they have slept in railway stations, and under bridges
For they have sharp elbows when it comes to a bargain
For all their meekness does not keep them from being cruel
For they will scratch at their itches until they are raw
For they regard the new and different with suspicion
For once they have accepted it, it becomes traditional
For they will happily be intoxicated by noon
For so they discovered gravity

For they will tell you they are the envy of the world
For they will not be fooled into signing up, not on your nelly
For the Holy Ghost is made in their image
For their own name for themselves is Lords of the Air
For they coo to the beggar woman as if they love her
For they remember when you got thruppence back on pop bottles
For they have The Knowledge
For they are robbed by the magpies in their sharp suits
For they complain bitterly of small discomforts
For they keep the real pain to themselves until it is too late
For they have gone hungry to feed milk to their children
For they cannot agree, even among themselves
For their history is a desert of day upon day
For no music is as pleasing to them as the sound of their own voices
For in their lives nothing has ever come easy
For from his high ledge the falcon has marked them out
For else they die quietly and the neighbours don't miss them
                                                    for months
For they are my brothers and sisters, being also made of dust.

THE LIFE OF BEES

The life of bees is like a magic well – von Frisch

If their speech is a dance –
                as formal and stylised as any Javanese court
or Tamil temple –

        then this loose bouncing jive
                                between the blue
                and blue
                        of lavender and thyme

    must be jazz song   or a kind of poetry:
a talismanic chant
                    out in the bright, cold, unconfined grave
        of the world.

                And if they must quit, again and again
    the perfumed darkness of ten thousand sisters

        it is to haul the sun
                            bucket by bucket   back
    to the sunless golden frame
                                whose frugal mathematics
            they fill with summer days
                    to make their dancing floor.

THAT THE BODY ALLOWS ITS PASSENGER
LIMITED ACCESS

And that the honeybee sees two colours beyond blue
or can distinguish the scent of each bell of the heather;

that the night sky is a roaring torrent of manifold fire;
that the far galaxies sing to us, most ravishingly, and that

the sun rings out like a bell from a city of many spires;
that the world is nothing that we perceive, because the body

is a bunker where the timid vainglorious self peeks through
its narrow slit in the hijab of the flesh, half blind, half deaf,

a crippled thing: of this, no doubt. And for this, gratitude,
that we go through the glory of things almost insensible.

How else could we live, when the light of dusk and dawn
and the marsh bird's call, and the apple crispness of frost
at its fancy ironwork already burn too much to bear?

BUDDLEJAS

Where the holes in the world are
these gypsies come
with their small gold eyes

and their bright coats
of foreignness – maroon
and purple.

All the places you're told
you should not go –
railway embankment

bomb-site, broken wall
of factory or tenement –
they make their camp.

The sweetness of their airs
plays over brick and glass
in summer sessions, all

beesong and the tablature
of leaf-vein wings. Their words
are written in an alphabet

too blue for seeing.
The ones who make the rules
want to root out their companies

because they dance
with the unruly seasons
and do not belong

to anyone but themselves
and the children of hive
and field follow them.

CUTTINGS

This year I forgot to prune
the whitecurrant
in time to get new wood

and so, although I love
its bark of brown slubbed silk
and the magician's handkerchief

of its unfolding leaves
(a green violent as spring)
this year it won't be hung

with those earring clusters
of tart and musky berries
gorgeous as opals.

It gives me pause
to think on what I've done
and haven't done

on what I am. What work
compares with a life?
And so, although I've loved

and planted as I can
there's still a toll to pay
for all those fruitful worlds

across the quantum foam
where this year, this evening
I've read stories to the kids

I'll never have
given them goodnight hugs, breathed in
their drowsy sweetness

now press berries to the lips
of a phantom wife.

THE WRITING MASTER

Let us consider how to form your m's, *madonna*
the high, sprung arch making a window
into a wider place; ah no, a little higher
for the best curve, parting from the body so
as if your nib were dancing a pavane. Remember
what we do depends on rhythm, and on these good
materials: China ink scented with musk and amber,
a swan's quill, fitting the wife of such a wealthy lord.

Come, let me lay my hand on yours to guide it right.
The pen has marked your gentle flesh, I fear.
Long years forcing black words onto the white
have calloused mine – can you not feel it, here?
Oh, sweet *madonna*, write words in m for me:
marriage; boredom; mischief; complicity.

THE BODY IS AN INGRATE.
IT DOES NOT REJOICE

in the abundance it is given. It gorges
because it does not believe in the future,
only in all that it has made or taken.

I will tell you how it is with the body.
It is a fierce, failed state. Oh the body is no
stranger to violence. It knows no mercy.

It has never yet wept for any stranger.
And yet, some do come, and find a home.
The body is not so singular as it supposes.

And others come, saying: the body is rich.
Let us take from it what we wish and cast
it down, because it is greedy and evil.

But the body will burn its own fields to ash
rather than cede to them. It acknowledges
only its own laws, its own terrible desires.

MODESTY

The world follows you home
                              a big dumb dog
            with its smells
and those caramel eyes
  in which can be read
                so many invented histories –

I too have known abandonment.

Animals recognise your greatness of soul –

but you know in your heart
        it just recognises a soft touch:
                there is no call
            for you to be in the photos.

Presently the dog will go
        haring off after some invisible prize
thrown by another hand

leaving you to hang
        in the deep well of stars.

RAVENSBOURNE

Another bone-legged evening with its long bill
waiting to swallow a little more of your life,
its wings a shadow on the river in which the shapes
of so many undone things are clearer to the gaze.
Snagged in a grief too extravagant
not to be mocked, snug on the rack of your own bones,
you cannot sense the medium in which you swim.

Mediocrity leaves small marks under the heart
and a taste like copper in the mouth;
there is no way to get from here to there.
Rain's texts vibrate on windows set to silent:
r u there? r u coming home? But everybody knows
those roads are drowned. The heron's on the wing.
The water is empty. The water is empty.

FALL

Numb rain; a wind rendering account
out of the unforgiving north

and the stubborn blossoms of the old fuchsia
have fallen at last to lie

with the slant days and the burnt letters.
Piled along the white fence, scarlet, deep violet

silk. The stiffened sepals, tiny frozen wings –
a massacre of hummingbirds.

SNAIL SONG

Like old hodmedod,
bellyfoot, silvertrail,
I want to fold myself
away from the world
and its too-many teeth.

Inside my whorl
of deliberate dark
I would remember light
at my own pace.
I tire of all this life.

THE BODY WISHES TO BREAK FREE

and is becoming something
I no longer know, half-broken,
trembling with fear of the weight
on its back. It yearns to trample
its weak, appropriate loves, eager
to taste everything one last time.

It wants to tell the beautiful boys
that they are beautiful, the men
how strong and admirable they are.
The words shiver behind its lips
where a bone fire is burning
that turns the whole world to ash.

FLEETING BEAUTY

Even unliving things are granted it.
Silver, copper, so brave and bright
before tarnish and verdigris.

And the indescribable hues
just before dusk, in the purl of sky
over lion-coloured hills

or the blue dayfire trapped
in the failing ice, never quite true
on the canvas of memory.

So why should we be surprised
if the sight of youth, lithe and taut
as sails on the horizon, steals our wind

or we are moved to kiss the slack, soft
peonies of an old woman's cheek?
All we lose is no more than we have.
But it hurts. How much it hurts.

LEVANT

There is a hill of pines, which is the incense of the day,
there is a garden of jasmine, the incense of the night,
there is the white silence of noon when the dogs dream.

There is sulphur and salt, the shattered mosaic of the sea,
the shark's jawbone of the hills, cinnamon-violet –
and you and I on either side of the days' widening stream.

Let all the books be ash, charred scraps of soot that flee
the beggar's clutch of air, languid and violent;
black as the small coffees served in endless stream

so that we may drink – me in the empire of day,
you, restless, in the desert kingdoms of night –
and you forget history, and I remember how to dream.

THE BODY CONSIDERS WHAT IT WOULD
BE LIKE TO BE A WHALE

to glance with a small eye from the mountain of its bulk,
and return the half-remembered embrace of water. It holds
a store of bullion in the red-curtained chambers of its lungs
and unparalleled mastery in the blowing of bubbles.

The body does not imagine. It reacts, moment by moment,
yet uncounted moments are written in its flesh. Somehow
it anticipates a last music, the hiss-thump of the ventilator
like waves on a shore to which it dare not come too close.
And somehow it knows how it is to spread fins like wings

in order to hang, head down, in the resounding depths
and allow its loneliness, its aches, all its long-drawn burdens
to transmute into song, an ululating groan and squeal
that echoes from the drowned peaks, down to the grey
and lightless plains where the dead dream asphodels.

YAQUT AT HIS EXERCISES

Write, Yaqut, in your high tower,
though the smoke of burning books
might make a man weep.

Write, and the reed in your grasp
remembers water.

This scrap of linen
on which you write
is all you can save

save the burnished reed in your grip,
the ink in its pad. So write, Master

in the script *meticulous*.
Ignore the screams and the song
of the double-curved bow.

Do it over in *copyhand*;
in stately *thirds*, celebrate unity.

Write, and believe:
though the knife you bear
cuts only pens

letters will form a sea
the fiercest horseman cannot cross.

Perfumed-like-basil,
scrappy, downfall.
Fill the white void.

Let *mim* and *ya* unfold under your nib
like the Euphrates flowing out of Paradise.

Write as you must, Yaqut,
even yet, with a cramp
in the brown bay of your hand.

AND THEIR ARMS AROUND ME
LIKE A SHAWL

It's late November, season of the dead. In the office
people are 'let go': we watch them fall, knowing
we can't catch them.
                              Over the bridge each night
the crow-host of umbrellas straggles homewards,
reflected tail-lights from the queues of traffic
gleaming under their feet – they trample on poppies.

But at midday against a blue deep enough to burn,
the banners of the maple blaze in the leaf-strewn park
and the joy of the colours is sudden and tender as pain:
an embrace from my own dear dead, whose blessings
spiral onto my shoulders in their generous end.

Such moments are surely grace,
                                        undeserved gift
of the world's grounding, even though I can't believe
in talismans, or heaven, or the persistence of love.

FORAMINIFERA

the Bearers of Holes

These fretwork polygons beneath the lens
are simple plankton with a lovely name.
Their constant rain of stars into the deep
will form the limestone of the days to come.

The craftsmen of al-Andalus who shaped
that stone in Kufic letters, leaf and briar
in sunwarmed spirals on the palace walls
knew that the pattern's made by what's not there.

They would have learned, like us, a way to bear
the holes the days have left; but maybe depth
and time alone can teach us how to forge
an absence into art, loss into strength.

PRAYER

When did my mother of the liquid eye
become a bird, a cage of hollow bone
and feathers frail beneath my hand?
Bird, come sing to me, as you have done
through so many summers.

And when did my father come to fit
so easily in the circle of my arm?
God grant them trees, beautiful trees
to offer shelter, and bright coats of many days
to keep them from the compass of the wind.

AESCULUS

The fruit is less formidable than it first appears,
its spikes too blunt for anything but show.

In its suede heart it cups the sheen and polish
of so much labour. We call it conker
because it reminds us of small victories.

When we grow old it soothes our fragile veins,
even as it kills us with the poison, nostalgia.

GIFTS

Because to love and be loved
is the most precious thing,
we should be profligate,
like those ancient kings
whose hands overflowed with gold.

So before my vault is closed
                    I give you these days
with their jade border of trees
gilded by the morning.
Wrapped in a sky of the singing blue
that comes only from lapis
of the highest grade.
                    And to you

I give these manuscripts:
the blue-black vellum of night
on which I have written
in silver and my finest hand
the character for 'stars'
ten thousand times.
                  To her

a golden chain of memories
and laughter, to hold her white ships
before they set sail.
                    And to them,

garlands of flowers, always,
because they will take no more
and deserve no less.

                    But to you all, the keys
to the fortified town called my heart
with its crooked streets
and a fine castle, where you can see
to the bright line of the horizon.

CALLIGRAPHY CLASS

The sun is ruling lines through the window,
waking chalk ghosts on the board, a palimpsest
of Roman capitals with their architecture of hidden rules.

The nib recites its complaints to the paper,
which is firm and a little uneven under my hand.
My ink smells of memories: incense, a lover's hair

sometimes cheap coal and cats' piss, the smell
of winter mornings when Dad knelt in patient service
at the hearth, gas poker like a T written in blue flame.

And what we do is dancing, only very small:
the sun has come to join us in our measures
writing over and over the one word, Life.

Notes

Lex(is) – Lex means 'law' in Latin, but the Greek 'lexis' has been used by linguists to describe speech considered as meaning, in contrast to 'praxis', which is speech considered as action.

Schwa – the name for that neutral mid-central vowel sound common in English (and many other languages), like a in about. The turned e, ə, is its official symbol in the International Phonetic Alphabet.

Buddlejas – or buddleias. The taxonomists have changed the familiar name, a phenomenon distressingly common for gardeners these days.

Yaqut at his Exercises – The great Muslim calligrapher, Yaqut al-Must'asimi, during the sack of Baghdad by the Mongols, is said to have retreated to the top of a minaret, where he calmly carried on his daily writing practice.

PAUL BLAKE lives in London and works as a medical writer. He has had short stories and poems published in a variety of magazines including *Iota*, *Brittle Star*, *Poetry Scotland*, *Scheherazade* and *Altair*. His poetry has also appeared in the anthologies *This Little Stretch of Life* and *Said and Done*, and he regularly reviews for *Brittle Star* magazine. His poem 'Triboluminescence' was highly commended in the Forward Prize for Poetry.

If you've appreciated and enjoyed this book, perhaps you'd like to write a review for us either on Stonewood's own website at www.stonewoodpress.co.uk or on the seller's website if you bought it elsewhere.